Who Was Walt Whitman?

by Kirsten Anderson

illustrated by Tim Foley

Penguin Workshop

To Juniper, who is the journey-work of stars—KA

For Keenan and Lydia—TF

PENGUIN WORKSHOP
An Imprint of Penguin Random House LLC, New York

Visit us online at www.penguinrandomhouse.com.

Library of Congress Cataloging-in-Publication Data is available upon request.

ISBN 9780399543982 (paperback)   10 9 8 7 6 5 4 3 2 1
ISBN 9780399543999 (library binding) 10 9 8 7 6 5 4 3 2 1

Contents

Who Was Walt Whitman?

It was a hot day in July 1854. The photographer Gabriel Harrison stood in the doorway of his Brooklyn studio, watching the people pass by on the city street. Suddenly, he recognized a friend. He called out and asked him to come in for a photo session. His friend hesitated.

Harrison called again. "Do come: come: I'm dying for something to do."

His friend was interested in photography and liked being in photo studios. Photography was still a very new technology. He went in and let Harrison take his picture.

A year later, Walt Whitman was getting ready to publish a book of his poems called *Leaves of Grass*. Walt didn't put his name on the cover as the poet. Instead, he just included a picture of himself inside. He chose Harrison's photo from that summer day. In *Leaves of Grass*, the poems didn't rhyme. Many were written about things that nice, polite people didn't talk about at that time, like relationships and the human body. People were shocked. *Leaves of Grass* was not like other poetry, and some people didn't even consider it to be poetry at all.

For many, the photo of Walt was just as surprising as the poems. Poets were supposed to look elegant and thoughtful. They would wear a jacket and tie—respectable clothing. But Walt Whitman was dressed like an ordinary workingman. He wore an open-neck shirt and rough pants. He had on a battered hat that was tilted down over one eye. And he certainly didn't look like he was dreaming up delicate lines of poetry. He had one hand in his pocket and one on his hip. He stared into the camera defiantly.

Years later, Walt would say he wasn't sure about the photo. He thought he looked angry, like he was "hurling bolts at somebody." But he also admitted that he liked it because it was "natural, honest, easy."

Walt's poems were supposed to be for everyone, including the working people who dressed like he had in the picture. Walt wanted to be a poet for all Americans. In order to do that, he had to change the way poetry was written. He had to create a new way of writing that matched the energy and diversity of the young nation.

Walt kept revising *Leaves of Grass* throughout his entire life. In some editions, he used more traditional photos of himself. But in most versions, he included the Harrison picture. It made the most sense. It was the photo that matched his style of groundbreaking poetry the best.

No one expected that Walt Whitman would be the person who shook up American literature.

He had been a newspaper editor, journalist, and printer. He had written a novel that even he thought was very bad. But he had been preparing his whole life to become this new kind of poet. Ever since he was a young boy watching people rush by on the busy streets of Brooklyn.

CHAPTER 1
Long Island to Brooklyn

Walter Whitman Jr. was born on May 31, 1819, in West Hills on Long Island, New York. His parents were Walter and Louisa Van Velsor Whitman. He was the second child in the family and was always called Walt. His brother Jesse was one year older than him.

Six more children followed: Mary, Hannah, George, Andrew, Jeff, and Eddie. The younger children looked up to Walt and considered him the leader of the family. Walt was very close to his mother. He thought she told wonderful stories.

The Whitman family had once owned a lot of land on Long Island, but they no longer did by the time Walt was born. His grandparents still had a farm, though. Walt would sometimes ride on his grandfather's cart as they delivered fruit and vegetables to the market.

Walt's father was a carpenter. In 1823, he moved the family to the nearby city of Brooklyn, which was growing very quickly. Walt's father hoped to be able to make money by building and selling houses. But Walter Whitman Sr. was not a very good businessman. He lost more money than he made. He struggled to support the family. They moved seven times in ten years.

But there still were good times. When Walt
was six, the Marquis de Lafayette, the great
Revolutionary War hero, marched in a parade
in Brooklyn. Lafayette had been born in France
but had come to America as a young man to
join the fight for American independence. The

Declaration of Independence had been signed less
than fifty years earlier, and some of the heroes of
the American Revolution were still being honored.
As Lafayette paused to greet people on the street,
he stopped, picked up Walt, and kissed him. Walt
told this story for the rest of his life.

New York City, Manhattan, Brooklyn

Today, the term "New York City" includes five boroughs: Manhattan, Brooklyn, the Bronx, Queens, and Staten Island. These boroughs each have their own character, but they are all a part of one big city. However, back in Walt Whitman's day, when people said "New York City," they meant only Manhattan.

Manhattan is an island, with the Hudson River to the west and the East River to the east.

Brooklyn is across the East River from Manhattan, and when Walt was growing up, it was its own city. It grew so fast during his lifetime that by 1860, it was the third most populated city in the United States!

Brooklyn and Manhattan were closely connected, though, with ferries regularly carrying people from one to the other. That is, until 1883, when the Brooklyn Bridge was completed, allowing people to ride or walk across the river.

Manhattan had long been America's most populated city, but in the late nineteenth century, Chicago began to threaten its place at number one. In order to remain America's biggest city, Manhattan, Brooklyn, Staten Island, parts of Queens County, and a part of Westchester County known as the Bronx joined together to form New York City. The city's population instantly grew to over three million, keeping it safely ahead of its Midwestern rival.

Walt began to go to a local school when he was around six. Outside of school, he spent a lot of time wandering around the busy, growing town of Brooklyn. Walt took in all the people, sounds,

and smells around him. He loved riding the ferries that ran across the East River from Brooklyn to Manhattan. He visited his grandparents on Long Island and swam in the ocean.

Walt quit school when he was eleven years old to get a job. First, he worked as an office boy for a group of lawyers. One lawyer helped him with his handwriting and got him a membership at a library. Walt read as much as he could. He discovered a whole world of novels and poetry. He felt that this was the most important thing that had ever happened to him.

Next, Walt became a printer's apprentice. He learned to lay out the pages of a newspaper, set the pieces of metal type, and then print them on large sheets of paper. Working on a newspaper gave him a chance to see the power of words. As he learned about setting up the press, he also read the articles. He observed what went into writing a good piece and how editing could make it better.

The Whitman family moved back to Long Island in 1833, but fourteen-year-old Walt stayed in Brooklyn. He finished his apprenticeship in early 1835 and then began working as a printer in Manhattan. He began to write, too, and he was thrilled to have some of his pieces published in New York papers. But after two huge fires hit the city's printing district, it was hard to find

work as a printer. Walt moved back to Long Island to live with his family and eventually became a schoolteacher.

Walt's students liked him. But he wasn't very interested in the job. He sometimes spent his classroom time reading, writing stories, or just thinking. He was only seventeen years old. But he was tall and strong. He looked like a grown man.

In 1838, he decided to start his own weekly newspaper. He called it the *Long Islander*. Walt wrote the articles, edited them, and printed the paper. He even delivered the newspaper, riding around Long Island on his horse, Nina.

It was fun at first. But Walt didn't like sticking to a schedule. Sometimes, he liked to spend his days lying under a tree thinking or floating in the ocean off Long Island. Walt put out the newspaper only when he felt like it. The people who had given him money to start the paper had had enough. After ten months, they sold it.

Finally, in 1841, he decided that it was time to leave Long Island. He moved to the city—Manhattan.

CHAPTER 2
City Life

Walt worked as a printer and editor for the next few years. He also began to write seriously. He wrote newspaper articles and short stories. Some stories were good enough to be published by newspapers and magazines.

He also wrote poetry. His poems were the same kind everyone else was writing at the time. They had rhymes, and each line had the same rhythm. They were written in the same style British writers had used for centuries.

Nothing Walt wrote seemed special or different. But one newspaper editor liked his work enough to ask him to write a novel. The editor wanted a "temperance novel." These were popular stories that were meant to warn people about the dangers of drinking alcohol. Walt's novel *Franklin Evans, or, The Inebriate: A Tale of the Times* was published in 1842. Walt thought it was a piece of junk. But it sold twenty thousand copies!

Walt seemed more likely to succeed as a newspaper editor than a fiction writer or poet. He certainly dressed the part of an editor. He wore a fancy coat and tie, along with a fashionable hat. Like many gentlemen of the time, he carried a cane while out walking.

And Walt loved to walk. He walked all over the city, often when he should have been working. He watched the crowds of people rushing on the busy streets: deliverymen, carpenters, horse-cart drivers, lawyers, merchants, and shopkeepers.

Walt marveled at the rushing variety of people he observed as he strolled along the streets. They were all part of his city, constantly vibrating with energy.

Walt took in all the city had to offer. He went
to museums and libraries and attended lectures
given by popular speakers. He loved music,

especially opera. He enjoyed theater and thought
Junius Booth's performance in the play *Richard
III* was the greatest thing he'd ever seen.

The Booth Family of Actors

Junius Booth

Junius Brutus Booth was born in London in 1796. He began to act when he was seventeen, and he soon became one of Britain's most popular actors. In 1821, he moved to the United States and settled in Maryland. He found success, performing all over the country.

Junius's son Edwin started performing with his father when he was young. Edwin adopted a more natural style of acting and became successful on his own. Edwin's younger brother John also became an actor. He did well, though he was not considered as talented as his brother.

John considered himself a Southerner. When

the Civil War began, he sided with the Confederacy. He bitterly resented the Union, Lincoln, and what he saw as an attack on Southerners' way of life. The rest of the family sided with the Union. Edwin is remembered as one of the greatest American actors of the nineteenth century. John Wilkes Booth is famously remembered as the man who assassinated Abraham Lincoln.

John Wilkes Booth

GRAND DEMOCRATIC FREE SOIL BANNER

In the 1840s, new states were being created in the United States as territories petitioned for statehood. The country was divided on whether slavery should be allowed in these new states. Walt considered himself a Democrat, but the party was split on this issue. Some Democrats wanted to stop slavery. Others thought it should be allowed. Walt was against slavery. He became a member of the Free Soil Party, which demanded that slavery be kept out of new states.

In 1848, Walt met the owner of a New Orleans newspaper, the *Crescent*, who offered Walt a job as its editor. On February 11, Walt set off for New Orleans. He brought his youngest brother, Jeff, with him. He wanted to teach fourteen-year-old Jeff how to be a printer. Traveling by stagecoach, train, and steamship, it took two weeks for the Whitman brothers to reach New Orleans.

Walt loved New Orleans, another busy city filled with all kinds of people. But soon the editors became worried by Walt's politics. Slavery was accepted in New Orleans. Walt's Free Soil beliefs were not appreciated. At the end of May, Walt and Jeff returned to Brooklyn.

CHAPTER 3
Leaves of Grass

Walt still occasionally worked in printing and journalism. He also built houses to sell. He wasn't a carpenter, like his father, but he drew plans for the houses and hired the workers. He even built a house for his family on Myrtle Street in Brooklyn.

Walt may not have actually been a laborer, but he began to dress like he was. He got rid of his fancy coat, tie, fashionable hat, and cane. Instead, he put on rough clothes like a workingman. No one would have mistaken him for a newspaper editor.

But, new clothes aside, he was still a writer at heart. He was now focused on becoming a poet. In 1847, he began to carry a notebook with him, jotting down ideas and phrases in it. By 1854, he was turning them into poems. They weren't the same old type of poems, though. He was trying to invent something different.

The United States was still a young nation full of energy in the 1850s. New people were arriving all the time from other countries to accomplish exciting things. The country had busy cities, but it also had miles of open prairies, mighty mountain ranges, and wild seacoasts. Everything seemed new, and something was always being built or created.

Yet some said there were still too many old European traditions in this new country. Ralph Waldo Emerson was one of the great thinkers of the nineteenth century. In the 1840s, he argued that Americans were still copying European culture. Their poems, stories, and art were still too similar to Europe's. He said Americans needed a poet who wrote in a truly American style.

And Walt agreed with Emerson. He believed that the old style of poetry couldn't capture the fantastic diversity and energy of America. He also hoped that poetry could be used to unite people. Slavery was dividing Americans, and many people feared that the country would actually split into two. Walt thought that poetry could show Americans how much they had in common.

In 1855, Walt published a book of poems. On the green cloth book cover was the title,

Ralph Waldo Emerson (1803–1882)

Born in Boston, Massachusetts, Ralph Waldo Emerson studied to become a minister. But after the early death of his young wife, he began to question his beliefs. He felt that faith didn't have to come from a specific church  or religion. Instead, people could connect to God themselves. Emerson believed that a relationship with nature was an important part of spirituality. With others, he developed this into a philosophy that became known as Transcendentalism.

He became a popular lecturer and essay writer. He spoke about philosophy, nature, and the need for Americans to create their own culture and art. Other writers who were influenced by Emerson include Henry David Thoreau and Emily Dickinson.

Leaves of Grass. Inside was an engraving of Gabriel Harrison's photo of Walt dressed like a workingman. The only clue about the author's identity came in one of the poems, where he wrote the line, "Walt Whitman, an American, one of the roughs, a kosmos." *Kosmos* was a word used to describe all of outer space. Walt meant that he was both part of the universe and one with it.

The twelve poems were unlike any others written before. They didn't rhyme or have specific rhythms. Each was untitled, given just a number.

Some just seemed like lists of things, with long strings of lines that began with the same word, like a chant or a song. He wasn't writing poetry in the traditional way. Walt was writing in a new style that would become known as "free verse."

The subjects of the poems also were different. He wasn't writing about great heroes or describing beautiful places with elegant words. Walt wrote about everyday people doing everyday things. In one poem, he wrote:

I hear America singing, the varied carols I hear,
Those of mechanics, each one singing his as it
should be blithe and strong,
The carpenter singing his as he measures
his plank or beam, . . .

But he also wrote *for* them. Walt hoped ordinary folks would read his poems and see themselves in them, as well as see other Americans.

Free Verse

Free verse is a type of poetry that does not focus on rhyme or rhythm. It is written to be more like natural speech than classic poetry.

A traditional poem might have a specific number of beats per line. Each line ends with a period or comma, to show the reader where to pause. That helps create the rhythm. In free verse, the pauses—periods or commas—can come anywhere in a line. Each line can have a different rhythm or none at all.

Matthew Arnold

Some British poets in the nineteenth century, like Matthew Arnold, had begun to experiment with the style of free verse. But most people consider Walt Whitman to be the first free verse poet.

In some poems, Walt wrote about the human body in a very honest way. Walt took delight in the idea of the physical body, and he thought it was just as important as the soul. Many people at this time did not agree.

Everything about *Leaves of Grass* was shocking. Many readers didn't understand it or even know how to describe it. But the subjects Walt wrote about and the style he used changed poetry and American literature forever.

CHAPTER 4
Sprouting Leaves

Walt paid to have 795 copies of *Leaves of Grass* printed. Hardly any of them sold. It did get some reviews, but they were mostly negative. Some people hated the things he wrote about, like the human body. Others hated the new style

of his poems. Some people just hated all of it! But most people barely noticed it.

Some of the few positive reviews had actually been written by Walt himself! He submitted them to newspapers without signing his name. No one knew he had written them.

But one person did admire *Leaves of Grass*. That was Ralph Waldo Emerson. These poems were everything he had asked for in his lectures about America's need for its own culture. This was the kind of new, exciting writing that he had hoped to see.

Emerson wrote Walt a letter. He told him that he thought these were the best American poems he had seen. He said that he was greeting Walt "at the beginning of a great career" and hoped to meet him sometime.

Walt was thrilled. He admired Emerson, and he knew Emerson's approval was important. This was an opportunity. He let a friend who was a newspaper editor print the letter.

Walt then sent the newspaper clipping to other friends, well-known writers, and anyone he thought could give the book more attention.

Walt started working on a second edition of the book. He added twenty more poems and gave them titles instead of numbers. At the end, he included a copy of the letter from Emerson, plus a letter from himself back to Emerson thanking him. The spine of the book had the title and the quote from Emerson. "I Greet You at the Beginning of A Great Career. R.W. Emerson."

The new *Leaves of Grass* was published in 1856. Walt had a thousand copies printed. But he sold even fewer than the first edition, and he lost even more money.

Walt wasn't discouraged, though. Over the next few years, he wrote more and more poems. He also worked as the editor of the *Brooklyn Daily Times* for two years.

And he was now somewhat famous, at least to other writers. Authors and critics came to visit Walt in Brooklyn and also to spend time with him at Pfaff's, a tavern in Manhattan. It was a place where artists, writers, and actors hung out. They didn't live very traditional lives. As the author of the "shocking" *Leaves of Grass*, Walt seemed to fit right in.

Walt was hoping to find a publisher who would put out a third edition of *Leaves of Grass*, but no one seemed to be interested. Then, in early 1860, he heard from a new Boston publishing company called Thayer & Eldridge. They were young and excited about publishing different kinds of writing. They wanted to publish *Leaves of Grass*.

Walt rearranged and revised his older poems. Then he added 146 new poems to this edition. Many explored love, relationships, and the wonders of America. Others seemed to reflect how the United States was now in a difficult time. Since Walt's first edition of *Leaves of Grass*, the country had become even more divided over slavery. His poems expressed his fear about the state of the union.

Walt went to Boston to oversee the printing himself. He met Emerson there, who had seen the new poems. He told Walt he should take out the poems about love because people wouldn't accept them. He thought the book would be more successful without them.

Walt didn't take Emerson's advice. The book was published in May 1860 with all the poems.

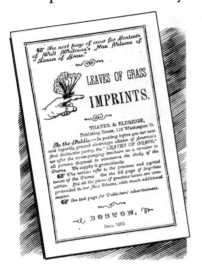

Thayer & Eldridge advertised the book, and it even got some good reviews. More copies were sold than the other editions. It seemed like things were going well. But at the end of the year, Thayer & Eldridge went bankrupt. They couldn't print any more copies of the book.

Walt was disappointed, but he didn't let himself dwell on it. His life—and the lives of all Americans—was about to change.

CHAPTER 5
Life during Wartime

On the night of April 12, 1861, Walt was heading home after the opera. Newsboys on the streets were waving special editions of their papers. Walt bought one and read it right there. Because of the slavery debate, seven southern states had left the United States. Now troops from one of them, South Carolina, had attacked Fort Sumter, which was run by US Army forces. The American Civil War had begun.

The American Civil War

The Civil War was fought between the Union, or Northern states, and the Confederate States of America, a group of Southern states that had seceded (left the union) after the election of Abraham Lincoln in 1860. The Southern states believed that Lincoln and the Republican Party hoped to end slavery. Southerners feared this would ruin their economy because the success of their plantations relied on the free labor of enslaved Black people.

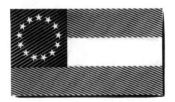

| Confederate States of America flag (1861–1863) | United States of America flag (1861–1863) |

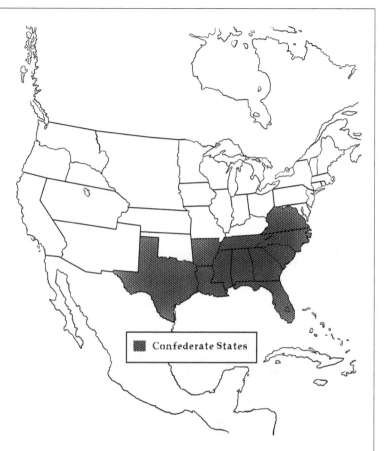

The war lasted four years until the Confederacy surrendered to the Union Army on April 9, 1865. About 620,000 to 750,000 soldiers died in the war. That is more than the number of Americans who died fighting in any other war.

One of Walt's brothers, George, fought for the North in the Union Army. His brother Andrew also joined, but he became sick and was sent home.

Walt and the rest of the family in Brooklyn read newspaper accounts of the war. They checked the lists of dead and wounded in the papers after each battle to see if they recognized any names.

In December 1862, they read about a battle in Fredericksburg, Virginia. George was listed as one of the wounded.

Walt left for Washington, DC, as soon as possible. He wanted to look for George in the military hospitals around the city. But he was robbed on the way and arrived in Washington without a penny. He wandered around the streets of Washington, trying to find information about George. After a few days, he ran into Charley Eldridge, one of the publishers of the 1860 edition of *Leaves of Grass*, and William O'Connor, a writer Walt had met in Boston. They gave him some money and helped him find George at an army camp in Virginia.

George only had a minor injury and was doing quite well. Walt stayed with George for nine days. He spent time walking around the camp, talking to the soldiers and observing their lives.

There was one sight at the camp that Walt never forgot. Outside of a makeshift hospital, he saw a pile of amputated limbs. There were legs, arms, and feet. All had been removed from wounded soldiers. They were too damaged for the doctors to repair.

Walt kept a notebook with his thoughts and observations. Some ideas were lines for poems. Some were for newspaper stories. George gave him details about the Battle of Fredericksburg. Walt turned them into an article for the *Brooklyn Eagle.*

Walt left the camp but didn't return to Brooklyn. Instead, he decided to stay in Washington, finding a job in the office of the army paymaster— the person who paid the soldiers and employees.

Walt had a reason for staying in Washington. After work each day, he would visit different hospitals, spending hours with the wounded soldiers. The busy nurses and doctors didn't have much time to give attention to the lonely soldiers. Walt took over that job.

Sometimes he read to the soldiers, and

sometimes he simply talked with them. He
answered their requests for things they wanted,
like candy or new shirts. Walt spent hours sitting
with them so they wouldn't feel alone. If a soldier
died, Walt often wrote a letter to his family, to
let them know about their son's, brother's, or
husband's last days.

It cost money to buy all the things the soldiers needed. And Walt didn't earn that much. People in Washington who heard about his work began to help him out. His younger brother Jeff, who was still in Brooklyn, also asked people for donations and sent them to Walt.

Walt was only in his forties, but his hair had turned gray, and he had a long, gray beard.

When he arrived at a hospital with his sack of cookies, jelly, paper, and stamps, he probably looked a bit like Santa Claus or a kindly grandfather. Some soldiers continued to write to him, even after the war had ended. Walt estimated that he may have met eighty thousand to one hundred thousand soldiers during his hospital visits. Many of them for the rest of their lives remembered the tall, gray-bearded man who had visited them in the hospital.

CHAPTER 6
The Good Gray Poet

In the summer of 1864, Walt became sick from exhaustion. Doctors advised him to take a break from his hospital visits, and he returned to Brooklyn to rest. While there, he got news that his brother George had been taken prisoner by the Confederate Army. The family would not hear from him again for months. Walt returned to Washington in January 1865. He had a new full-time job at the Department of the Interior copying letters and documents. For the first time in a long time, he had a job that would give him financial security. And he would still have time to visit the hospitals and write.

Walt visited Brooklyn again in April 1865. George had been released from prison by then,

and Walt was anxious to see him. He also was
preparing a new book of poems called *Drum-
Taps*. The poems were about the war and what he
had observed in the hospitals.

Then, on April 9, the war ended. Walt was still in Brooklyn with his family on April 14 when he heard the news that President Lincoln had been assassinated while watching a play at Ford's Theatre in Washington, DC.

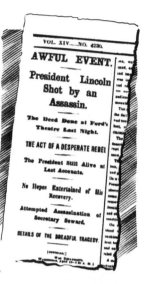

Walt was devastated. He had admired Lincoln and the way he had tried to hold the country together. He felt they shared the same ideas about America and democracy. Although they had never spoken, he had seen Lincoln in person a number of times. He felt a connection to him.

Abraham Lincoln
(February 12, 1809–April 15, 1865)

Walt walked out into the small garden behind his mother's house. He noticed that the lilacs were blooming. That image stayed in his mind, and he began to work on poems about Lincoln.

Walt returned to Washington and his job in the Department of the Interior. But the new secretary of the Interior found out that Walt had written *Leaves of Grass*. He read some of it and was horrified. He didn't want Walt working for him, and so he fired him. Luckily, a friend got him another job in the attorney general's office. Walt actually liked this job more, and he was happy about the change.

While in Washington, Walt published a book called *Sequel to Drum-Taps* with eighteen

poems, including some about President Lincoln. One poem was based on his memory of the lilacs in his mother's garden, called "When Lilacs Last in the Dooryard Bloom'd." Another, called "O Captain! My

Captain!" used images of a sea voyage and a ship's captain who had died. Neither of these poems mentions Lincoln by name. But people knew whom they were about.

Walt's friend William O'Connor was furious at the way Walt had been treated by the secretary of the Interior. O'Connor was a respected writer and editor. He thought Walt's work was brilliant and hadn't received enough attention. In 1866, he published a pamphlet called "The Good Gray Poet."

THE

GOOD GRAY POET.

A VINDICATION.

NEW YORK:
BUNCE & HUNTINGTON, 459, BROOME STREET.
1866.

O'Connor argued that Walt's poetry was an important work of American literature that captured real human experiences. He also pointed out that Walt was a good person who had helped many people during the war.

Not everyone changed their opinions about Walt's writing overnight. But William O'Connor's pamphlet made some people begin to rethink their ideas about Walt and his poems.

CHAPTER 7
Friends from Britain

Walt returned to New York in late 1866 to oversee the printing of a new edition of *Leaves of Grass*. For Walt, *Leaves of Grass* was a book that

was always changing. He wanted the words and the poems to reflect America. With the 1867 edition, he was trying to bring the experience of the Civil War into the book. The war was now part of America.

But Walt's work also appealed to people outside of the United States. Over the years, some people in Britain had become fans of Walt's work, and a British writer named William

Michael Rossetti reached out to Walt. He wanted to be the first to publish Walt's poems in Britain. But Rossetti wanted to make some changes.

He thought Walt should cut or change some words and ideas about how Walt felt about love and about the body—the same arguments people had with these poems earlier. Walt wanted his poems published to a greater audience outside the United States, but he also didn't believe in making those types of changes. Rossetti worked around that. Instead of changing the poems themselves, he just left out the ones that he thought might offend British readers.

Rossetti's book, *Poems by Walt Whitman*, was published in 1868. It spread Walt's work to a wider audience. Through Rossetti's book, Walt made some new British friends.

Many would support him and his work for the rest of his life.

Walt began to work on his own new edition of *Leaves of Grass*. The edition he published in 1870–71 had three sections devoted to the Civil War poems. He also included a few poems that dealt with Reconstruction, the era after the war, and America's need to move forward as a new nation. In 1872, he had the edition printed again. This time he

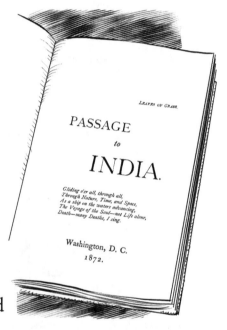

LEAVES OF GRASS.

PASSAGE
to
INDIA.

Gliding o'er all, through all,
Through Nature, Time, and Space,
As a ship on the waters advancing,
The Voyage of the Soul—not Life alone,
Death—many Deaths, I sing.

Washington, D. C.
1872.

included a section of poems called "Passage to India." These were about the wonders of modern technology and spiritual and physical journeys.

That year, Walt was invited to read a poem at Dartmouth College's graduation ceremony. He didn't know that the students had chosen him with the hope that he would read something that would shock their teachers! The poem

Walt read was not shocking, much to his young audience's disappointment. But Walt was flattered. He thought the invitation to speak at Dartmouth meant that his work was becoming more accepted.

CHAPTER 8
Camden

The year 1873 was a difficult one for Walt. In January, he suffered a stroke that left him partially paralyzed on his left side. He was fifty-four years old. In May, his mother became ill. Walt traveled to Camden, New Jersey, where she was living with his brother George and his wife. She died just a few days later. Walt had always been very

close to his mother. Even when he was living in Washington, they had written to each other constantly. Losing her was a terrible blow.

Walt returned to his job in Washington in the beginning of June, but he was still too ill to work and live on his own. He decided to move to the city of Camden and live with George. The city would become his home for the rest of his life.

Walt settled into his life in New Jersey. Camden was right across the Delaware River from Philadelphia, and Walt often visited the city.

In January 1876, an unsigned essay appeared in a New Jersey paper. It was about how Americans had not given enough credit to the brilliant poet Walt Whitman. It said that he had struggled to get published, and that people didn't bother to read or understand his work. It said that Walt, who had given so much to his country, was just struggling to get by.

Walt sent copies of the essay to his friends in Britain. That started an international literary debate. British writers wrote about how shameful it was that Americans didn't recognize their great poet. American editors argued back that they had treated Walt fairly. During this time, other critics went back to Walt's work and wrote new, more positive, and open-minded reviews of his poems.

It turns out that Walt had written the essay. It had gotten him the attention he had hoped for. He released a "centennial edition" of *Leaves of*

Grass. He said it was meant to go along with the celebration of the American Centennial—the one hundredth birthday of the United States. It sold better than any other edition of *Leaves of Grass.*

The sales of this edition meant a lot to Walt. The money he earned helped, but he also wanted people to read and appreciate his work. He still believed poetry was important and that a book like *Leaves of Grass* could make a difference in people's lives.

In 1876, Walt also published *Memoranda During the War*, a book of his essays and articles about his Civil War experiences. *Two Rivulets* was another book he put out that same year. It was a mix of poetry and essays. It also sold better than expected, thanks to his essay about himself.

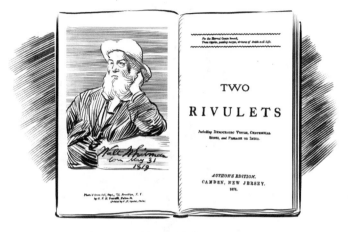

By 1879, Walt felt healthy again. He began to spend more time in New York City, where he gave the first of what became known as his "Death of Abraham Lincoln" lecture. In his speech, he talked about his personal memories of Lincoln. He gave a vivid account of Lincoln's assassination. Walt had not been present that night, but his good friend Peter Doyle had been at Ford's Theatre and had given Walt all the details. He talked about Lincoln's impact on America and finished by reciting "O Captain! My Captain!"

Walt was not a powerful speaker, but people seemed to like the speech. He would give it again in different places over the coming years.

That same year, Walt took a trip out west.
He thoroughly enjoyed the long train trip. He
thought it was amazing that he could go to sleep
in a comfortable bed in his sleeper car and then

wake up the next day in a completely different state. He enjoyed seeing the wide-open prairies of the Midwest, which were so different from the busy cities and dense forests of the East. He stopped briefly to visit his brother Jeff in St. Louis, where he was an engineer in charge of the city's waterworks, then traveled to Kansas, where he spent time with his fans and admirers.

By now, Walt was well-known enough to have readers who lived across the United States. Finally, he reached Colorado. He was thrilled by the natural wonders of the Rocky Mountains but also fell in love with the city of Denver. He even considered moving there but instead returned east.

Transcontinental Railroad

Trains began to operate in the United States in the 1830s. Railroad travel expanded rapidly, but it all happened east of Missouri. People who wanted to travel to the West Coast had to either take a dangerous overland journey by wagon or coach from Missouri to California, or a long, difficult sea passage around South America.

It was clear that there was a need for a railroad that stretched from east to west. Finally, in 1862, President Lincoln signed the Pacific Railroad Act to build a transcontinental railroad.

One company started building tracks from California, heading east. Another started at the Missouri River, building west. Thousands of Chinese immigrants worked on the railroad. It was a dangerous job that often required explosives.

On May 10, 1869, the two companies met at Promontory Summit in Utah. A final spike, made of gold, was driven into the tracks at 12:47 p.m.

It now took days instead of months to travel from the East Coast to the West Coast. The price of the trip dropped from $1,000 to about $150. The country was now truly connected.

CHAPTER 9
Banned in Boston

In 1881, James R. Osgood and Company, a Boston publishing company, offered to publish *Leaves of Grass*. Osgood was a respected company. It would pay all the expenses of printing and put the book in bookstores. It seemed like a big opportunity.

Walt spent a lot of time working on the new edition. He cut thirty-nine poems and added seventeen new ones. He revised others. He focused on putting clusters of poems that dealt with the same topic into an order that would make sense. By now, *Leaves of Grass* contained almost 293 poems.

Osgood published the book in October 1881. It sold more than fifteen hundred copies in the

first few months it was on sale. The 1881–82 edition of *Leaves of Grass* is often considered the best version ever published.

Then, in March 1882, James Osgood got a letter from the Boston district attorney. It stated that he considered *Leaves of Grass* to be "obscene literature." He meant the way Walt described

James R. Osgood

relationships between men and women. At that time, it was against the law to sell literature that contained details about such topics! If Osgood continued to publish *Leaves of Grass*, he would be charged with a crime.

The district attorney sent Walt and Osgood a list of changes that would need to be made in order for him not to bring charges. Walt considered making them. He wanted people to read his work. But he would have had to cut some poems entirely and lines from others.

He had been asked to do this before—to make
his poems more "acceptable." And he just couldn't
do it. He felt that would hurt the meanings of
the poems and the book.

Osgood reluctantly stopped publishing *Leaves of Grass*. But he gave Walt the metal printing plates he had used to create the book. That meant another publisher could print the exact same edition quite easily. Rees Welsh, a Philadelphia company, offered to publish it. The Philadelphia district attorney did not give them any trouble. And all the publicity helped sales. Over six thousand copies of the Philadelphia edition were sold.

In 1882, Walt also published *Specimen Days & Collect*. It contained his memories of different parts of his life. It included many of his pieces about the Civil War that had already been published. But it also had stories about his family and childhood, his observations about nature, and his trip to the west in

Specimen Days & collect

By WALT WHITMAN
Author of "LEAVES OF GRASS"

WILSON & McCORMICK, SAINT VINCENT STREET
1883

1879. Some chapters were just one paragraph long. It was the closest he would ever come to writing an autobiography.

Walt was now well-known enough that other famous people came to visit him. Oscar Wilde, the popular Irish playwright, spent an afternoon with him in 1882. In 1884, Henry Irving, who was considered one of Britain's greatest actors, came to visit Walt. Irving was introduced to Walt by his manager, who loved Walt's poetry.

The manager's name was Bram Stoker. In 1897, Bram Stoker published a novel about a cruel vampire called *Dracula*.

In 1884, Walt bought a house on Mickle Street in Camden. He had been living with his brother George and his wife, but George wanted to move out of the city. Walt wanted to stay. The Mickle Street house was the first he had ever owned. It wasn't fancy, but Walt didn't mind. It was home.

CHAPTER 10
Mickle Street

As Walt approached the age of seventy, his health was getting worse. In 1885, friends raised money to buy him a horse and carriage so that he could get around town more easily. Walt and his driver went out most days so Walt could see the countryside and get some fresh air.

During this time, a young man from Camden became one of his closest friends. Horace Traubel admired Walt's work. He helped Walt out any way he could and began to visit him almost every day. He started to interview Walt about his life and thoughts, and he wrote down everything he said.

Walt had other visitors, too, some old friends, some new fans. Photographers took his picture. The famous painter Thomas Eakins came to paint his portrait. It was Walt's favorite picture of himself.

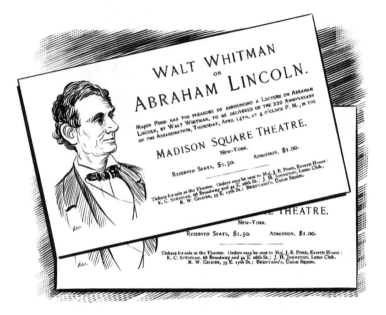

In 1887, Walt gave his Lincoln lecture for the last time at Madison Square Garden in New York City. The next year, he published another book of poetry, *November Boughs*. Soon after, he suffered a series of strokes. He was not able to go out as much after that.

But he kept writing. In 1892, he published a book of poetry and essays called *Good-bye My Fancy*. He also put out the final edition of *Leaves of Grass*.

Walt Whitman died on March 26, 1892. Horace Traubel was by his side. Over one thousand people came to his funeral, including friends and admirers from New York and Washington.

In the early 1900s, Traubel began to publish a series of books called *With Walt Whitman in Camden*. He had written down many of the conversations he had shared with Walt.

Traubel also started a monthly magazine called *The Conservator*, focusing on other people's writings about Walt's work. It helped keep readers interested in Walt's poetry.

The many editions of *Leaves of Grass* changed the way people thought about poetry. They showed that a poem didn't have to be a series of rhyming, even lines. They encouraged people to experiment with the art form. They also showed that poems did not have to be about grand, elegant people or fancy stories and ideas. They could be about anyone and everyone. And poetry could be *for* anyone and everyone.

Walt's work affected many other writers, including William Carlos Williams, Langston Hughes, Allen Ginsberg, and June Jordan. Walt's approach to poetry also encouraged painters and photographers to be more experimental. The famous architect Frank Lloyd Wright was influenced by him. He read his work aloud to his students. Composers such as Benjamin Britten, Ralph Vaughan Williams, and John Adams have set Walt's poems to music.

Walt's name can be found on schools and streets all across the United States. The Walt

Whitman Bridge links Camden to Philadelphia.
And there is even a Walt Whitman Service Plaza
on the New Jersey Turnpike.

Millions of people pass through these places. All kinds of people from everywhere. Walt was aware that everyone was different but that there was something that made people the same, too.

In "Song of Myself" he wrote, "I am large, I contain multitudes." He meant a person can contain many different thoughts, feelings, and ideas, and that sometimes they might not agree or make sense. But they still exist together. It is the same way he felt about the country he knew and believed in. The United States contained multitudes, and yet it was all one.

As Walt once said, it was like a poem.

Timeline of Walt Whitman's Life

1819 — Born May 31 in West Hills, Long Island, New York

1823 — Moves to Brooklyn with family

1831 — Becomes a printer's apprentice

1833 — Works as a printer in Manhattan

1838 — Writes, publishes, and delivers the *Long Islander*

1841 — Moves to Manhattan and begins to write fiction and poetry

1842 — Publishes *Franklin Evans, or, The Inebriate*

1855 — Publishes first edition of *Leaves of Grass*

1856 — Publishes edition of *Leaves of Grass* with Emerson letter

1860 — *Leaves of Grass* is published by Thayer & Eldridge

1863 — Moves to Washington, DC, to help wounded soldiers in army hospitals

1868 — William Michael Rossetti publishes *Poems of Walt Whitman* in Britain

1873 — Suffers stroke and moves to Camden, New Jersey, to live with his brother George

1876 — Publishes *Memoranda During the War* and "centennial" edition of *Leaves of Grass*

1879 — Gives first "Lincoln Lecture"

1882 — New edition of *Leaves of Grass* is banned in Boston

1892 — Publishes *Good-bye My Fancy* and "deathbed" edition of *Leaves of Grass*

Timeline of the World

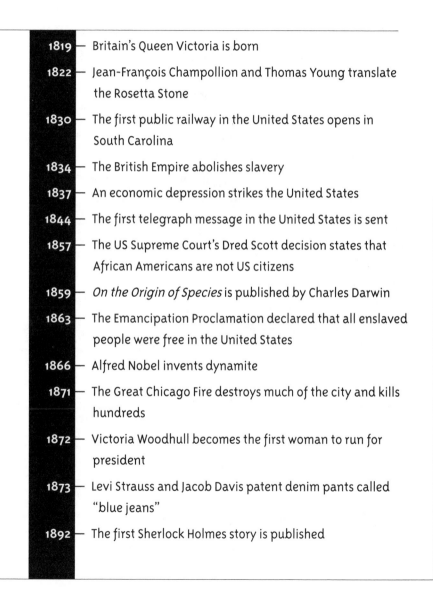

1819 — Britain's Queen Victoria is born

1822 — Jean-François Champollion and Thomas Young translate the Rosetta Stone

1830 — The first public railway in the United States opens in South Carolina

1834 — The British Empire abolishes slavery

1837 — An economic depression strikes the United States

1844 — The first telegraph message in the United States is sent

1857 — The US Supreme Court's Dred Scott decision states that African Americans are not US citizens

1859 — *On the Origin of Species* is published by Charles Darwin

1863 — The Emancipation Proclamation declared that all enslaved people were free in the United States

1866 — Alfred Nobel invents dynamite

1871 — The Great Chicago Fire destroys much of the city and kills hundreds

1872 — Victoria Woodhull becomes the first woman to run for president

1873 — Levi Strauss and Jacob Davis patent denim pants called "blue jeans"

1892 — The first Sherlock Holmes story is published

Bibliography

Kaplan, Justin. *Walt Whitman: A Life*. Perennial Classics: New York, 2003.

Martin, Justin. *Rebel Souls: Walt Whitman and America's First Bohemians*. Da Capo Press: Boston, 2014.

Reynolds, David S. *Walt Whitman*. Lives and Legacies. Oxford University Press: New York, 2005.

Roper, Robert. *Now the Drum of War: Walt Whitman and His Brothers in the Civil War*. Walker & Company: New York, 2008.

Whitman, Walt. *Specimen Days & Collect*. Melville House: Brooklyn, [1882] 2014.

Website

www.whitmanarchive.org